I Will Sing of the
Goodness
of God

An intentional journey of
knowing God's character

By Marjie Schaefer

www.FlourishThroughTheWord.com

ISBN: 979-8-9909136-5-3

I WILL SING OF THE
GOODNESS
OF GOD!

Welcome to this four-week journey of discovering more about the goodness of God.

The lyrics to the song by the same title are provided for you, and I encourage you to search various artists who sing this song. Watch their videos and worship along with them. This is a beautiful and powerful worship song and declaration of the truth of God's goodness.

This study is designed for you to do alone with the Lord, but you can also invite a friend or a group to join you and then gather to share your insights. Maybe you even have a long-distance friend who will want to join you, and you can plan a zoom or facetime call to share together.

The well-known author, Dallas Willard said, "The single most important thing in our mind is our idea of God."

My prayer is that your 'idea of God' will grow and strengthen as you devote your time to intentionally focus on His goodness.

This has been my prayer for myself. I want to stand securely on the truth of God's goodness, even when my circumstances may cloud my view of Him.

Set aside time each day to deepen your relationship and friendship with the Lord. You are on your own timetable to do this.

May God pour out His blessing as you study and learn from Him.

Your friend,

Marjie

Week One
of your
Journey

THE GOODNESS OF GOD

I WILL SING OF THE GOODNESS OF GOD

I love You, Lord
For Your mercy never fails me
All my days, I've been held in Your hands
From the moment that I wake up
Until I lay my head
Oh, I will sing of the goodness of God

And all my life You have been faithful
And all my life You have been so, so good
With every breath that I am able
Oh, I will sing of the goodness of God

I love Your voice
You have led me through the fire
In the darkest night
You are close like no other
I've known You as a Father
I've known You as a Friend
And I have lived in the goodness of God

And all my life You have been faithful
And all my life You have been so, so good
With every breath that I am able
Oh, I will sing of the goodness of God

Your goodness is running after, it's running after me
Your goodness is running after, it's running after me
With my life laid down, I'm surrendered now
I give You everything

'Cause all my life You have been faithful
And all my life You have been so, so good
With every breath that I am able
Oh, I'm gonna sing of the goodness of God
Oh, I'm gonna sing of the goodness of God

~: Jason David Ingram, Brian Johnson, Edmond Martin Cash, Benjamin David Fielding, Jenn Johnson.
For non-commercial use only

WEEK ONE: DAY 1

Read Exodus 33:12-19 out of the Amplified Version:

12 Moses said to the LORD, "See, You say to me, 'Bring up this people,' but You have not let me know whom You will send with me. Yet You have said, 'I know you by name, and you have also found favor in My sight.' 13 Now therefore, I pray you, if I have found favor in Your sight, let me know Your ways so that I may know You [becoming more deeply and intimately acquainted with You, recognizing and understanding Your ways more clearly] and that I may find grace and favor in Your sight. And consider also, that this nation is Your people." 14 And the LORD said, "My presence shall go with you, and I will give you rest [by bringing you and the people into the promised land]." 15 And Moses said to Him, "If Your presence does not go [with me], do not lead us up from here. 16 For how then can it be known that Your people and I have found favor in Your sight? Is it not by Your going with us, so that we are distinguished, Your people and I, from all the [other] people on the face of the earth?"

17 The LORD said to Moses, "I will also do this thing that you have asked; for you have found favor (lovingkindness, mercy) in My sight and I have known you [personally] by name." 18 Then Moses said, "Please, show me Your glory!" 19 And God said, "I will make all My goodness pass before you, and I will proclaim the Name of the LORD before you; for I will be gracious to whom I will be gracious, and will show compassion (lovingkindness) on whom I will show compassion."

1. What did Moses base his appeal to God on in this recorded conversation? Write out the verse here.

2. Have you ever had a similar conversation with the Lord? Have you reminded the Lord of the things He has promised to you? Tell about one of your prayers here and how the Lord responded to you.

3. Do you think Moses had the credibility to 'negotiate' with God? Why or why not?

4. Look up Psalm 103:7 and write out the verse here. Expand on what you learn from this dialogue between Moses and the Lord.

5. Wrap up your study time today by listing at least three (3) ways the Lord has displayed His goodness to you today.

Re-read the text provided in Day One: Exodus 33:12-19. Ask the Lord to speak to you through His Word. Use this text to answer the questions below.

1. What do you learn about the relationship between Moses and the Lord from this passage?

2. Write out your favorite verse of dialogue that Moses said to the Lord here.

3. How does the Lord respond to Moses? What do you learn from this conversation?

4. Why do you think it is important to spend time on this passage before doing a deeper study on the goodness of God? Base your answer on scripture.

5. Take the time to write out your gratitude to God for His goodness to you today.

Week One: Days 3 & 4

For the next two days, you will be utilizing this passage of scripture by doing **verse mapping.**

What is verse mapping, you ask?

Verse mapping is a method of studying the historical context, translation, connotation, and theological framework of a verse (or section) of the Bible. In other words, verse mapping gives you the opportunity to get real about studying the Bible.

The exercise of verse mapping over the course of these next two days will give you the opportunity to do more than just read the Bible. You have unlimited time to research and apply what's in the Bible to your life today.

Verse mapping is for anyone who wants to know the Word of God more. Is that you? If so, let's get started!

For each section, be sure and read the directions as you complete each part.

Verse:

For our purposes in this study, we will be using the following verse to map: Exodus 33:19.

Write out Exodus 33:19 here and include the translation you use:

Design:

Write Exodus 33:19 in two to four different translations here. Underline or highlight the key words or phrases that stand out to you from the various translations.

How do the different translations present the same idea or biblical principles?

$\mathcal{D}$EVELOP:

Look up the key words or phrases that you marked. Use a concordance or online word search to discover the meanings of your key word or phrases and write them down. If a word is used across all translations, find out why. Tell why and how the verse, key word, or idea is important through the Hebrew language. (Dig deeper!)

As you view this verse in context, think like a storyteller—how would you explain what is happening in your verse? Step into the character's shoes (Moses in this case). Look what happened before and after your verse.

$\mathcal{A}$CTION:

Write out the following from your study:

What is happening in the verse?

Who are the characters?

How does this story relate to other areas of Scripture? Glean other Biblical references as you study and look those up to answer this question.

Don't be afraid to read more in Exodus to get the 'full meal deal' of this passage and verse!

OUTCOME:

Summarize what you've learned from this journey and study of this verse. The outcome should reflect whatever truth has been revealed in your map. This is where you would make personal application.

WEEK ONE: DAY 5

Today you will end your week of study by meditating on Psalm 103.

Look up this psalm in several translations and choose your favorite, or the one that resonates with you the most.

Read through the entire psalm once and then read it out loud.

Spend time on verses 2-4 especially and take the time to write out three ways you can bless the Lord and remember His benefits. This is your time to write out your gratitude to God for His goodness.

> *Lord, grant that I may always allow myself to be guided by You. Grant that in all things, great and small, today and all the days of my life, I may do whatever You require of me. Help me respond to the slightest prompting of Your grace, so that I may be Your trustworthy instrument for Your honor. May Your will be done in time and in eternity by me, in me, and through me. Amen.*

Week Two

THE GOODNESS OF GOD

We first hear the word *goodness* in Genesis 1:3 when God looked at what He created and declared it was good. The entire Bible cannot be exhausted when we dive into the Lord's goodness. His goodness is everywhere we look. In Exodus 33, we see how the Lord reveals His goodness to Moses with His presence.

Today's study on goodness barely scratches the surface, but we will look at a few verses that highlight the goodness of God and will end with a personal testimony—mine and yours!

1. Look up and write out each verse, then take the time to practice and declare exactly what each verse says:

   • 1 Chronicles 16:34

   • Psalm 23:6

   • Psalm 34:8

   • Psalm 107:1-2

   • Psalm 139:5

   • Psalm 143:5

2. How do you share the goodness of God with others?

3. How do you experience the goodness of God?

4. What are some ways you intentionally cultivate an attitude of goodness to others? Use Micah 6:8 to answer.

God's promises are far more potent than our problems! His goodness far exceeds anything difficult that we endure.

We can anticipate and look forward to the wonderful ways God moves and works in our lives.

1. Look up Romans 15:13 in several translations. Write out your favorite here.

2. How can you develop a practical habit of hope? Use the verse above to help you answer this question.

3. Every day we can know that God's goodness does not change just because our circumstance or seasons of life may change. Look up each verse below and write out what each one says and tell how you can apply it practically in your life today and develop the habit of hope.

    • Psalm 147:3:

    • Romans 8:37:

    • Ephesians 2:10:

    • Romans 8:18-19:

In the book of Jeremiah, God has told us that we are blessed and wise to make Him our hope and our confidence. When we trust Him more than we trust our circumstances, we learn to thrive in every season.

1. Read, ponder, and write out the highlights from Jeremiah 17:5-8.

2. From your reading of this passage, what does the Bible tell us about ways that we can stunt our own growth in the Lord?

3. In contrast to not growing, how does this scripture passage encourage you to grow in the Lord? Write out the specific ways you can cultivate your own growth in God.

4. Look up Isaiah 40: 31 and Isaiah 43:19. Write out each verse and list the specific instructions given to you as you continue to cultivate a habit of hope in God.

God wants us to anticipate His goodness and to live our lives with a holy expectancy, believing He is always up to something good.

1. God's hold on you is firmer than your hold on Him. Read Hebrews 6:18-19 in several translations. Write out your favorite version here.

2. What are the two things you read in the verses above that are unchangeable about God?

3. Based on the Biblical study you have done so far, how do you think the Lord intends to empower you and awaken you further to the reality that He is on your side and working for you?

4. Read and write out Proverbs 18:21, Proverbs 12:18, and Proverbs 15:4. How are the words you speak cultivating a habit of hope in God's goodness for you? Is there a habit you need to change or avoid? What practical steps will you take to steward your words and to intentionally cultivate a habit of hope in God's goodness?

This was not on my vision board!

On April 20, 2024, I arrived a few hours before our final Spring Flourish event would be happening. Many weeks of planning and preparation had gone into our luncheon for 250 women. We planned to gather in community, worship the Lord together, hear the stories of two new books being released, and focus on the personal importance of being in the Word of God each day.

I had many things on my to-do list before the doors opened, and so, to provide comfort as I walked around the church to do the many things, I decided on flip-flops for the win!

I was so busy and preoccupied doing the myriads of things (while comfortable in my flip-flops), I missed a step and took quite a tumble and landed on the floor.

I could tell immediately that the fall was a hard one, but I thought if I just recovered on the floor for a few minutes, I would be okay. I was wrong! To make a very long story short, I ended up having a terrible three-way break in my ankle requiring surgery and a hospital stay.

This was my first broken bone ever! I came out of surgery with a huge cast and strict directions not to put any weight on it for weeks.

Needless to say, this unexpected surgery and recovery radically changed my life. In fact, the entire ordeal canceled my life for about twelve weeks. Things I had planned, trips I had booked…. all was canceled and taken off my to-do list.

As soon as I began to realize the seriousness of my injury, I sensed the Holy Spirit reminding me that my response to this unplanned event would be everything. The precious Holy Spirit used this incident to cause me to reflect on the goodness of God amid hardship and injury.

The enemy's primary goal is to separate man from God. He will use anything to do this.

If I were to allow my injury to put distance in my relationship with the Lord, I would be on the losing end of everything.

My life was absolutely canceled for weeks, but Jesus met me at every turn and He showed me that God is bigger than a broken ankle! I learned that if I didn't fight Him regarding what had happened to me, but rather, surrender to Him in the midst, He would provide a peace and a joy I had never known.

No, this wasn't on my vision board, but I realized the Lord is still good even with a canceled life, a huge cast, daily discomfort, and weeks of not walking.

His goodness is revealed in His Presence and that is how I coped through twelve weeks of being sedentary. God is good.

Susie Larson, author of Waking up to the Goodness of God, writes:

> "God wants to move us out of bracing for impact and into a lifestyle of anticipating His goodness. He wants us to live with holy expectancy and believe He is always up to something good. Whether we perceive it or not, God is in the process of redeeming our story."

Use this day to write your own testimony of how God is redeeming your story. Prayerfully reflect on a time in your life (either past or present) where you counted on the goodness of God to help you through a difficult or unplanned situation.

Include in your story specifics of the Lord's goodness to you and to others. Also be sure to include the things you learned from this time in your life.

How are you living with holy expectancy and believing God is always up to something good?

Week Three

THE GOODNESS OF GOD

Week Three: Day 1

God's goodness is meant to inspire us to go out into the world and reveal His goodness to everyone we meet. His goodness is present everywhere, no matter what we are facing. We only need to let the Bible saturate our outlook on life, according to what it has to say about God's goodness.

1. Read the following verses and write out how you recognize and respond to the goodness of God in your life:

   • 2 Corinthians 3:18

   • Romans 2:4

   • Psalm 23:6

   • Psalm 27:13-14

   • Psalm 31:19

   • Psalm 34:8

   • Psalm 100:5

- Lamentation 3:25

- Jeremiah 29:11

- Romans 8:28

- Romans 12:21

2. Based on your study of these verses today, take the time to go back and re-read what you have written out. Pray through them as you go, asking the Lord for greater insight into His promises and His goodness.

Go back and re-read all the verses of scripture you looked up yesterday.

As you do this, choose two that especially spoke to you and resonated with your heart in your own personal pursuit of deepening your grasp of the goodness of God.

Once you choose your verses for today's study and tomorrow's, use the verse-mapping for an expanded study of the specific verses. The specific instructions are provided for you here again. Use this space or your personal journal to write out your insights from your study.

Verse:

Write out your chosen verse here and include the translation you use:

Design:

Write the verse in two to four different translations here. Underline or highlight the key words or phrases that stand out to you from the various translations.

How do the different translations present the same idea or biblical principles?

DEVELOP:

Look up the key words or phrases that you marked. Use a concordance or online word search to discover the meanings of your key word or phrases and write them down. If a word is used across all translations, find out why. Tell why and how the verse, key word, or idea is important through the Hebrew or Greek language. (Dig deeper!)

As you view this verse in context, think like a storyteller—how would you explain what is happening in your verse? Step into the character's shoes if this applies in your verse. Look what happened before and after your verse.

ACTION:

Write out the following from your study:

What is happening in the verse?

Who are the characters?

How does this story relate to other areas of Scripture? Glean other Biblical references as you study and look those up to answer this question. Don't be afraid to read more in the passage you chose to get the 'full meal deal' of this passage and verse!

OUTCOME:

Summarize what you've learned from this journey and study of this verse. The outcome should reflect whatever truth has been revealed in your map. This is where you would make personal application.

> *Breathe in me, O Holy Spirit, that my thoughts may be holy. Act in me, O Holy Spirit,*
> *that my work may be holy. Draw my heart, O Holy Spirit, to love what is holy.*
> (a prayer from St. Augustine)

God intends for you to flourish. Your flourishing can help others to thrive too. The Lord desires for the world to be nourished by your anointed, appointed, abiding-in-Christ life. He wants your soul to be free. The Lord's plan is for your life to be so miraculous that many see your life and put their trust in the Lord. (*Adapted from Waking up to the Goodness of God, by Susie Larson.*)

1. The psalmist in Psalm 40 knew the importance of waiting on and trusting in the Lord. Read Psalm 40:1-3 and write out scripture verses here.

2. From this psalm, what did the psalmist specifically do in his interaction with the Lord?

3. What did the Lord specifically do as listed in Psalm 40?

4. What conclusions can you make from this brief study of Psalm 40?

5. What do you learn about the goodness of God from this psalm?

Your agreement with the Word of God matters greatly in your daily walk with Him and as you seek to grow in the knowledge of His goodness.

1. What does Romans 8:6 tell us about our minds?

2. How is your mind today? Do you sense a level of peace and life in your soul? Are you feeling troubled? Bothered? Anxious? Take some time to pray about anything that is on your mind today or anything possibly weighing you down.

3. What promise did Jesus make in Luke 10:19? What does it mean for you in your daily life?

4. What do you learn from Matthew 12:25 and John 16:13? How can you practically apply these verses in your daily life?

A prayer from Susie Larson, Waking up to the Goodness of God:

> *"Loving Father, thank You for Your Son! Jesus, thank You for defeating sin and death on the cross for me. Thank You for winning a sound victory over the enemy. Because Your Spirit is alive I me, I am seated with You. Insecurity is just an illusion. I can't be more secure than I am right now. Help me live bravely and boldly and say no to every lie that trespasses against me. It's Your truth that sets me free. Awaken me today to the reality of Your goodness and the abundance of life I possess in You. Amen."*

Week Four

THE GOODNESS OF GOD

WEEK FOUR: DAY 1

God wants you to flourish! He is near you; He is for you; He brings good to you.

1. Read and write out Psalm 16:7-8. What are the two specific things you can do to apply this psalm?

2. Read Psalm 19 in its entirety. Read it aloud and use several translations as you do this. Write the truth about God as you spend time in this psalm today and list them as bullet points in the space provided.

3. Psalm 19 is a passage that expresses listening to and heeding the Voice of God. Jesus also had something to say about hearing His voice in John 10:27-20. Write out the specifics of what you learn from Jesus about listening to Him in this passage. How are your listening skills?

WEEK FOUR: DAYS 2 & 3

The well-known reformer, pastor, and author, Martin Luther, developed a way of praying called the four golden strands. His method of praying encouraged followers of Jesus to pray a verse of Scripture four ways.

FIRST: ask God to help you apply the verse to yourself in as many ways as possible. Remember—this is a prayer, not a self-beat-up.

SECOND: make appropriate confessions to God based on the applications from strand one.

THIRD: thank God for anything related to the verse's truth.

FOURTH: offer requests of God regarding the truth of that verse.

For the next two days of study, use the four-strand method of prayer on the following scripture passages: Psalm 23 and Matthew 6:9-13.

Take the time each day to sit quietly with the Lord, praying through the passages according to the four-strand method.

It will also be very helpful to you to write down the truths, applications, and requests you discover in each passage.

WEEK FOUR: DAY 4

As we near the end of this four-week study, hopefully you are seeing in a fresh, new way that you are wired for purposeful faith build on the infallible promises of God and His goodness. With that said, what are you believing God for?

Take the time to write it down here:

1. Explain (from the Word) the meaning of Psalm 37:4.

2. Do you believe that if you walk intimately with God and treasure His Word in your heart, He will shape your desires to match His desires for you? If so, how will God prepare you to steward the dream and confirm His will and His way to you?

3. Write out Ephesians 2:10 and explain what the truth of this verse means for you in your daily walk with Christ.

4. Ephesians 3:20 is an amazing promise made to God's children. Write the verse out here and summarize the personal meaning and application of it in your life after four weeks of focus on the goodness of God.

Week Four: Day 5

Today is the conclusion of your intentional study and focus on the goodness of God.

Take the time today to review your entire study (yes, all four weeks!) and revisit your favorite verses and prayers.

1. Choose one verse to write out in summary here of your most special lesson from God's Word as you studied:

2. Take a spiritual inventory of the goodness of God in your life over the past four weeks. Write out the specific ways you became more aware of His goodness. Thank Him for His specific answers to prayer in your life and His obvious activity in your life.

3. Let your mind fill with gratitude and your soul fill with peace as you focus on God's love and goodness to you. Write out Psalm 116:7 and spend time in prayer with this verse as your anchor.

4. Pay it forward: has there ever been a time when someone in your life was amazingly good to you? What did that feel like? How did it impact your heart? If possible, write them a note of thanks and let them know. If you cannot do that, be sure and tell the story to a friend.

The Word

What a wonder it is.

It will light your way in the darkness.

It will calm your anxious heart, heal your wounds, warn you of danger,

Protect and cleanse you from sin and make you wise.

It will bring you joy.

It is bread. It is water.

It is a counselor. It is life.

It is satisfying. It is sufficient.

It is supreme. It is supernatural.

It will lead you to Christ, the living Word.

And the sight of Him will change you forever.

~Nancy DeMoss Wolgemuth/ReviveOurHearts.com

Works Cited

The Amplified Bible, Grand Rapids, MI: Zondervan Bible, 1983. Print.

Cambron, Kristy. Verse Mapping Journal Bible Study. Harper Christian Resources. 2020. Print.

Larson, Susie. Waking Up to the Goodness of God. Nashville, TN. W Publishing. 2024. Print.

Schaefer, Marjie. The Fruit of the Spirit. Flourish through the Word. 2024. Print.

Wolgemuth, Nancy. "The Word". Revive Our Hearts.com.

ABOUT THE AUTHOR

Marjie Schaefer was born in Georgia, raised in Texas, and has spent the past four decades in Washington State. She and her husband, Steve, have been married for 36 years and have four grown children and two grandchildren.

Marjie describes herself as an everyday girl who loves Jesus and daily pursues a life with Him at the center of her activities and purposes.

She started leading and teaching Bible studies while a student at Washington State University and has continued to open her home and her life to anyone who wants more of the Word and more of Jesus. Her greatest passion is bringing the Word of God to life through practical application and visual tools. Women look forward to her personal touches while attending her studies, and they usually go home with tangible reminders of God's love for them.

Marjie started spending deliberate and daily time in the Word of God while she was a young girl at the encouragement of her godly mother. This has given her a foundation that has stood the test of time. She began writing her own Bible studies at the request of some friends who desired to study the Word during the summer months.

Marjie and her team currently lead the ministry, Flourish Through the Word, a 501c3 organization which is a community of women in the greater Seattle region committed to being equipped through God's Word. As a result of their time together in the Word, the women move out into their arenas of influence, shining their light for Jesus. You can find out more about this ministry, upcoming events and Bible studies at www.flourishthroughtheword.com.

ABOUT THE ARTIST

Desiree Jane Currier is a self-taught soft pastel artist based in sunny Phoenix, Arizona. Her work blends impressionism with emotion, dreamy skies, quiet landscapes, and the kind of light that lingers.

A boy mom and first-generation Filipino American, Desiree found her way back to art in the in-between moments of early motherhood. Pastels became her therapy, her joy, and her way of turning everyday scenes into something sacred. She loves to romanticize the ordinary and find beauty in the quiet corners of life.

Desiree is drawn to the soft, velvety texture of pastels...and the magic of not using a paintbrush, but instead blending with her hands. It's an intimate process, a conversation between her skin and the paper, full of feeling and presence.

You can explore more of her work, read the stories behind each piece, or collect your own original at _www.desireejane.com_.

Follow along on Instagram:@desireejanecurrier

Art for the soft-hearted and sky-eyed.

Other Flourish Bible Studies by Marjie Schaefer

A 5 week Bible study exploring the promised peace of Jesus.

Based on Galatians chapter 5, this 6 week Bible study will take you on a deep study of the fruit of the Holy Spirit.

A five week study that features the conversation of Jesus with His disciples in the gospel of John chapters 14, 15 and 16.

A 5 week journey on grace, truth, the Holy Spirit, and our identity, starting with the Gospel of John.

Spend four weeks on biblical principles of friendship, exploring commitment, communication, and community through Scripture.

Explore 1 Peter, focusing on faith, hope, love, and practical Christian living through a five week personal study.

The letter of 2 Peter focuses on spiritual disciplines and intentional growth through Jesus' provision for living in truth.

A six week study on how God's Word transforms us, guiding us to flourish spiritually and joyfully.

Learn how investing in others and recognizing their worth through biblical disciple-making principles is a life-giving key.

Other Flourish Bible Studies by Marjie Schaefer

A seven-week study inviting deeper relationship with God through biblical stories, declarations, and gratitude journaling.

This five-week study in James focuses on practical wisdom and spiritual growth through daily biblical reflection.

Explore how personal stories fit into God's Kingdom by studying the book of Habakkuk and the life of David.

This six-week study highlights the bravery of Abraham, Mary, the mother of Jesus, Peter and John, Paul and Silas, King David, and the woman at the well.

This five-week study examines biblical stories of faith and courage, offering encouragement and guidance for facing fear.

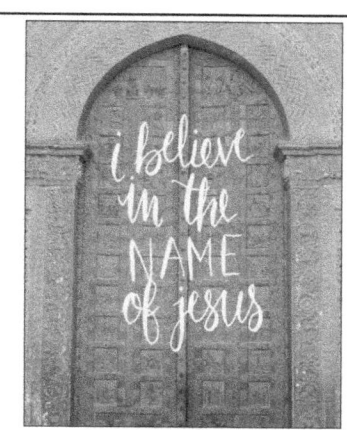

A study of the seven "I AM" statements of Jesus, exploring their significance and impact.

Walk through the book of Ephesians, focusing on Christ's majesty and practical daily living through Paul's biblical prayers and teachings.

Explore how to flourish through life with Jesus at the center, focusing on joy, renewal, and practical teachings from the book of Colossians.

A four-week study of Philippians, teaching how to find true joy through gratitude and knowing Jesus as we rise above our circumstances by grace.